# SEVERE STORMS

## Measuring Velocity

Greg Roza

# PowerMath™

The Rosen Publishing Group's
PowerKids Press™
New York

Published in 2007 by The Rosen Publishing Group, Inc.
29 East 21st Street, New York, NY 10010

Book Design: Michael Tsanis

Library of Congress Cataloging-in-Publication Data

Roza, Greg.
  Severe storms : measuring velocity / Greg Roza.
     p. cm. — (Math for the real world)
  Includes index.
  ISBN 1-4042-3366-0 (lib. bdg.)
  ISBN 1-4042-6085-4 (pbk.)
  6-pack ISBN 1-4042-6086-2
  1. Storms—Juvenile literature. 2.  Speed—Juvenile literature. I. Title. II. Series.
  QC941.3.R69 2006
  551.55—dc22
                              2005015498

Manufactured in the United States of America

# CONTENTS

# WHAT IS VELOCITY?

Have you ever noticed speed limit signs while you were riding in a car? These signs tell drivers how fast they are allowed to drive. For example, a sign that says "Speed Limit 55" tells drivers that the speed limit on this road is 55 miles (88 km) per hour. This is a measure of speed, or the rate of motion of an object, such as the car you're riding in. Scientists and mathematicians call speed a **scalar quantity**. This means that speed is a measure of **magnitude** alone. When we talk about speed, we say things like "fast," "slow," and "motionless." We also use specific units to define speed, such as "55 miles per hour."

People often confuse speed with velocity because they are nearly the same thing. Speed is a measurement of the rate of motion. Velocity is a measurement of the rate *and* direction of motion. This makes velocity a **vector quantity**, or a measure of magnitude in a specific direction. We express velocity as a measure of change in position during a unit of time in a specific direction, such as "55 miles per hour, north." Scientists use the term "displacement" to refer to the total change in position when dealing with velocity.

**speed:** A measurement of the rate of motion, or the distance moved over a unit of time.

**velocity:** A measurement of the displacement of an object in a specific direction.

**displacement:** The difference between the original position of an object and its new position; a change of position.

SPEED LIMIT 55

Distance is a scalar quantity that describes how far an object has moved.

5

Since speed and velocity are so closely related, it is helpful to understand how to calculate average speed before discussing average velocity. Average speed is calculated using the following **formula**:

$$\text{average speed} = \frac{\text{distance traveled}}{\text{time}} \qquad s = \frac{d}{t}$$

Let's say that you just finished a cross-country car trip. On the last day of the trip, it took you 9 hours to drive 495 miles (796 km). What was your average speed for this part of the trip?

Use the amounts above to fill in the formula for average speed.

average speed = 495 miles ÷ 9 hours

average speed = 55 miles per hour

On the last day of your trip, your average speed was 55 miles (88 km) per hour. You may not have driven 55 miles per hour the whole way. You might have driven 50 miles (80 km) per hour for a while and 60 miles (97 km) per hour for a while, but your *average* speed was 55 miles per hour. Your speed at any one moment during the trip—such as 58.5 miles (94 km) per hour—is called your **instantaneous** speed.

As we've seen, average speed is calculated by dividing the distance traveled by the time it took to travel that distance. Velocity is calculated by dividing the object's displacement—the difference between its final position and its original position—by the time it took to make that trip.

| | | |
|---|---|---|
| v = average velocity<br>d = displacement<br>t = time<br><br>$v = \frac{d}{t}$ | Another way to write this formula is average velocity equals the ending position minus the starting position (displacement), divided by the ending time minus the starting time. | $p_1$ = starting position<br>$p_2$ = ending position<br>$t_1$ = starting time<br>$t_2$ = ending time<br><br>$v = \frac{p_2 - p_1}{t_2 - t_1}$ |

START

495 MILES

9 HOURS

END

Notice that the formula for average velocity looks much like the formula for average speed. It is important to remember, however, that a velocity measurement always includes a direction.

7

Let's use the same situation from page 6 to calculate your average velocity. Assume that you are traveling east throughout the entire trip.

$p_1$ = starting position = 0 miles

$p_2$ = ending position = 495 miles

$t_1$ = starting time = 0 hours

$t_2$ = ending time = 9 hours

$$v = \frac{495 \text{ miles} - 0 \text{ miles}}{9 \text{ hours} - 0 \text{ hours}} = \frac{495 \text{ miles}}{9 \text{ hours}} = 55 \text{ miles/hour, east}$$

When an object is traveling in a straight line, its average velocity is the same as its average speed with the direction added.

Let's say that you've already traveled 1,000 miles (1,609 km) on your trip. You leave Houston, Texas, at hour 12 of your trip and travel due north to Tulsa, Oklahoma. Once you arrive in Tulsa, your entire trip has lasted 20 hours, and you've covered a total of 1,440 miles (2,317 km). What is the average velocity for the last part of the trip? Let's use the formula for average velocity to find out.

1,000 MILES; 12 HOURS

1,440 MILES; 20 HOURS

Velocity that is always the same or constant is called uniform velocity.

$p_1$ = starting position = 1,000 miles

$p_2$ = ending position = 1,440 miles

$t_1$ = starting time = 12 hours

$t_2$ = ending time = 20 hours

$$v = \frac{1{,}440 \text{ miles} - 1{,}000 \text{ miles}}{20 \text{ hours} - 12 \text{ hours}}$$

$$v = \frac{440 \text{ miles}}{8 \text{ hours}}$$

$$v = 55 \text{ miles/hour, north}$$

Tulsa is nearly due north from Houston, so your *average* velocity would be 55 miles per hour, north.

Remember that velocity is a measurement of rate of change in position and direction. Since this is true, you might be wondering what happens to our velocity calculations when we are not traveling in a straight line. Let's say that it took you 8 hours to drive 110 miles (177 km) north, 110 miles east, 110 miles south, and 110 miles west. What was your total distance? What was your average speed? What was your displacement? What was your average velocity?

To find the total distance, simply multiply 110 miles by 4.

$$
\begin{array}{r}
110 \text{ miles per part} \\
\times \quad 4 \text{ parts of the trip} \\
\hline
440 \text{ miles}
\end{array}
$$

You drove a distance of 440 miles.

To find the average speed, you can use the following formula:

$$ s = \frac{d}{t} $$

$$ speed = \frac{440 \text{ miles}}{8 \text{ hours}} = 55 \text{ miles/hour} $$

Your average speed was 55 miles per hour.

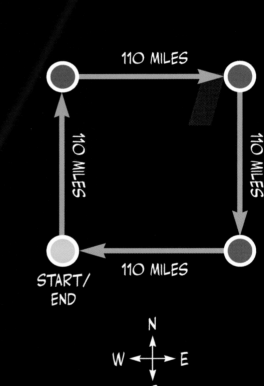

You changed directions several times during your trip and ended up back where you began, so your displacement—your final distance from your original location—is 0 miles. Your average velocity for the trip would be:

$$v = \frac{0 \text{ miles (ending position)} - 0 \text{ miles (beginning position)}}{8 \text{ hours (ending time)} - 0 \text{ (beginning time)}} = \frac{0}{8} = 0$$

At the end of the 8-hour trip, you ended up exactly where you had started; you experienced a displacement of 0. This means that you had a velocity of 0, even though you were moving at 55 miles per hour for 8 hours. When you have a velocity of 0, there is no indication of direction.

Let's say that you drove 110 miles (177 km) east. Suddenly you realized that you forgot your suitcase at the hotel! Then you had to drive 110 miles west back to the hotel to get your suitcase. From there, you drove 220 miles (354 km) east and decided to stop for the night. The entire trip took you 8 hours. What was the total distance that you traveled? What was your average speed? What was your displacement? What was your average velocity?

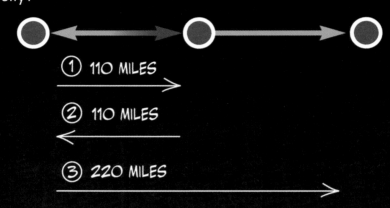

① 110 MILES

② 110 MILES

③ 220 MILES

To find the distance traveled, add up the 3 parts of the trip.

$$
\begin{array}{r}
110 \text{ miles} \\
110 \text{ miles} \\
+ \ 220 \text{ miles} \\
\hline
440 \text{ miles}
\end{array}
$$

You traveled a total distance of 440 miles.

To calculate your speed, use the formula for average speed: $s = \frac{d}{t}$.

$s = \dfrac{440 \text{ miles}}{8 \text{ hours}} = 55 \text{ miles/hour}$

Your average speed was 55 miles per hour.

Your displacement is the final distance that you were from the starting point. By looking at the map, we can see that your displacement was 220 miles. Now you can use the displacement to calculate your average velocity.

$$v = \frac{220 \text{ miles}}{8 \text{ hours}} = 27.5 \text{ miles/hour east}$$

Your average velocity was 27.5 miles per hour, east.

These examples help us see the differences between distance and displacement, and speed and velocity. However, automobile travel is not the only area of life where velocity is measured. Meteorologists—people who study and predict the weather—also need to measure and record velocities using data from a computer as shown below. This information can help us decide what to wear, plan activities, or stay out of the way of a severe storm.

13

WEATHER VANE

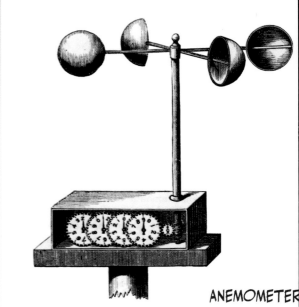
ANEMOMETER

# MEASURING THE WIND

Wind velocity is the direction and speed at which the wind is moving. Scientists use several different instruments to determine wind velocity. The simplest of these tools is commonly called a weather vane, which is made of a thin strip of wood or metal that rotates on a rod when the wind blows. The strip points in the direction that the wind is blowing.

An anemometer (aa-nuh-MAH-muh-tuhr) uses cups that spin around a rod with the wind to measure wind speed. Sometimes a computer records the motion of the cups to measure wind speed. A different kind of anemometer measures wind speed using a glass tube. Wind blowing into the tube creates pressure inside of it, which can be used to compute wind speed.

If you watch the local weather report on television, you have probably heard the term "Doppler radar." Doppler radar sends radio waves out from an **antenna**. The waves bounce off objects in the air—such as raindrops, snowflakes, hailstones, dust particles, and even insects—and return to the antenna. Doppler radar converts the data that it receives into pictures that show the position, strength, and movement of **precipitation**. Doppler images can show how fast and in what direction a storm is moving, which helps meteorologists predict where the storm will be within a few hours.

The meteorologists in this picture are keeping an eye on a severe storm in Kansas using Doppler radar.

Scientists use various methods to display data regarding wind velocity. A wind rose is a circular table that shows typical patterns of wind speed and direction at a specific location for a period of time, such as a month. It is marked around the circumference with compass directions and contains **concentric** circles representing percents of time. Bars that radiate from the center like the spokes of a wheel record wind direction. The length of each bar or spoke indicates the percent of time the wind blows from that direction. The colored bands within each spoke show the percent of time the wind from that direction blows within a certain speed range. For example, a wind rose may show that the wind from the northwest blows at speeds between 3.34 and 5.4 meters per second about 10% of the time.

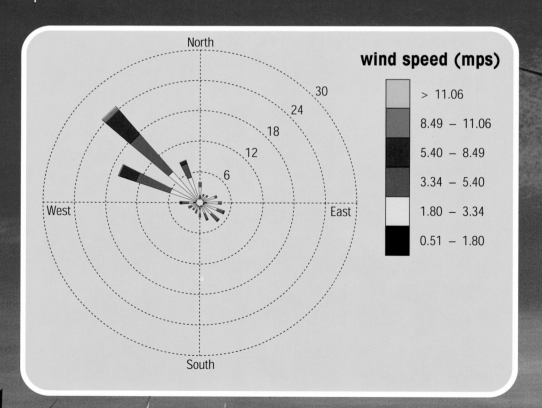

wind speed (mps)

> 11.06

8.49 – 11.06

5.40 – 8.49

3.34 – 5.40

1.80 – 3.34

0.51 – 1.80

Not only do wind roses help scientists find the direction from which the strongest winds blow in a specific location, they also show the directions from which little or no wind blows. This can be helpful when erecting **wind turbines**, allowing them to be positioned so they face the windiest direction. Wind turbines use the wind to make electricity. The wind turns the blades of the turbine that spin a shaft connected to a generator. This process creates electricity. A group of wind turbines can make electricity that is sent to an electrical grid, providing electricity to many homes and businesses in an area. Wind roses help to find the best locations for wind turbines. Meteorologists will continue to use wind roses to track wind currents and predict the weather patterns for a particular location.

Pictured here is a row of wind turbines located at Castle River Wind Farm near Pincher Creek in Alberta, Canada.

17

# THUNDERSTORMS

One of the most common kinds of storms is a thunderstorm. Thunderstorms need 3 conditions in order to form: warm, moist air in the lowest levels of the **atmosphere**; cold air in the upper atmosphere; and something to cause the warm, moist air to rise. One of the ways that warm, moist air is formed is when the sun warms the ground, causing the air just above the ground to heat up. When this happens, the warm air rises into the upper atmosphere where the air is colder. Moisture in the warm air cools in the upper atmosphere and forms a cloud. This cloud may continue to grow if warm, moist air continues to rise. Added moisture causes water droplets to form. When clouds get too heavy with water, rain falls. Gradually, an electrical charge builds up in the cloud. This charge is released as lightning, which we hear in the form of thunder.

Most thunderstorms are about 15 miles (24 km) across and last for about 20 to 30 minutes. Thunderstorms can be rather mild, or they can be very dangerous. The 2 greatest dangers associated with thunderstorms are lightning and flash floods caused by sudden, abundant rainfall. A severe thunderstorm is one that produces hailstones at least $\frac{3}{4}$ inch (1.9 cm) in diameter and has winds of at least 58 miles (93 km) per hour.

Wind shears are sudden and often severe changes in wind velocity. The downward wind shears associated with thunderstorms are called microbursts. If a microburst originates 15,000 feet (4,572 m) in the air and reaches the ground in 5 minutes, what is the velocity of the microburst?

18

Use the formula for average velocity to find the answer.

$$v = \frac{d}{t}$$

$$v = \frac{15,000 \text{ feet}}{5 \text{ minutes}}$$

$$v = 5 \overline{\smash{)}15,000}^{\,3,000} \text{ feet per minute}$$

The wind in the microburst is traveling at a speed of 3,000 feet per minute. How do we change this scalar quantity to a vector quantity? That's right, we add a direction. The velocity of the microburst is 3,000 feet per minute, down.

Wind shears can be dangerous for airplanes. A microburst can cause an airplane to quickly change speed and direction. Pilots call these atmospheric disturbances "turbulence."

# DUST STORMS

Dust storms are caused by turbulent winds—rough winds that change direction randomly—blowing over dry land that has little or no **vegetation**, such as deserts. Dust storms can also occur over land that has suffered from a lack of rain, widespread overgrazing, or poor farming methods. Turbulent wind causes larger dust particles to tumble along the ground. Smaller particles sometimes bounce high enough to be held up by the wind as it rushes past. These particles—most of which are less than $\frac{1}{400}$ inch (0.0635 mm) in diameter—remain in the air until the wind dies down or until they hit a solid object. Some dust storms can cover thousands of miles. For example, dust storms that begin in the Sahara in Africa can carry dust particles out over the Atlantic Ocean and sometimes as far as Brazil in South America!

Severe dust storms make travel impossible because they can reduce **visibility** to zero. Dust particles can sting the skin and even chip paint off cars and homes. Frequent dust storms are a major cause of soil **erosion** in certain parts of the world. Objects in the middle of dust storms can be completely covered by soil before the storm moves on.

Let's say that a dust storm, starting at point A on the map below, had traveled 200 miles (322 km) east in 5 hours when it reached point B. Eight hours after the storm began, it reached point C, which was a total of 320 miles (515 km) east of point A. Find the average velocity of the dust storm from point B to point C.

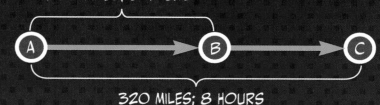

200 MILES; 5 HOURS

A ————→ B ———→ C

320 MILES; 8 HOURS

Use the information in the text to fill in the formula for average velocity.

$$v = \frac{p_2 - p_1}{t_2 - t_1}$$

$$v = \frac{320 \text{ miles} - 200 \text{ miles}}{8 \text{ hours} - 5 \text{ hours}}$$

$$v = \frac{120 \text{ miles}}{3 \text{ hours}}$$

$v = 40$ miles/hour

$p_1$ = starting point (B) = 200 miles

$p_2$ = ending point (C) = 320 miles

$t_1$ = starting time = 5 hours

$t_2$ = ending time = 8 hours

The storm moved an average of 40 miles (64 km) per hour between points B and C. To make this scalar quantity a vector quantity, we need to include the direction: 40 miles per hour, east.

During the 1930s, the states of Colorado, Kansas, New Mexico, Oklahoma, and Texas were plagued by ongoing dust storms that were the result of overfarming and overgrazing. This area became known as the Dust Bowl. The dust storms were eventually controlled in part by planting new forests to block the wind from blowing over farmland.

# BLIZZARDS

A blizzard is a severe winter storm with winds traveling 35 miles (56 km) per hour or more. These winds carry snow with them, causing visibilities of less than $\frac{1}{4}$ mile (0.4 km) for at least 3 hours. Most blizzards include heavy snowfall, sleet, and freezing temperatures. This combination often results in "whiteouts," or periods of low to zero visibility. Strong winds can also cause a windchill. This means the wind causes the air temperature to feel colder than it actually is.

Blizzards are similar to thunderstorms. It is common to see lightning and hear thunder during a blizzard. When freezing air passes over a body of water that has not frozen, the moist, warm air can rise into the developing storm clouds, just as it does during the formation of a thunderstorm. The freezing air turns the moisture in the warm air to snow, sleet, or freezing rain. When this is combined with strong winds and freezing temperatures, a blizzard can become dangerous, especially for people who are traveling.

Let's say that a blizzard had a velocity of 35 miles (56 km) per hour, northeast, when it formed. An hour later, it was still traveling northeast, but its speed had increased to 65 miles (105 km) per hour. Let's assume that the **acceleration** of the blizzard was constant during this time. What was the average velocity of the storm over this hour?

During a blizzard, high winds can push fresh snow across the ground, making driving very dangerous.

We already know the velocity of the storm when it began—35 miles per hour, northeast—as well as its velocity after an hour—65 miles per hour, northeast. Since the storm accelerated at a constant rate, all we have to do is add the 2 velocities and divide by 2 to get the average velocity.

```
   65  miles/hour, northeast
+  35  miles/hour, northeast
  100  miles/hour, northeast


      50  miles/hour, northeast
2 ) 100
```

The blizzard's average velocity was 50 miles per hour, northeast.

A tornado is a swiftly rotating column of air that forms beneath a thundercloud. The swirling wind of a tornado reaches down to the ground and, if it is strong enough, destroys much of what it touches. Most tornadoes travel about 35 miles (56 km) per hour and last for only a few minutes, but they can leave a path of destruction that is about 1,500 feet (457 m) wide. The most devastating tornadoes can be about a mile (1.6 km) in diameter, travel about 70 miles (113 km) per hour, and last longer than 1 hour.

A tornado touches down at point A. It takes 4 minutes to travel through points B and C, and end at point D. By adding up the distances on the map, we can see that the total distance the tornado traveled was 4 miles. Four miles in 4 minutes equals an average speed of 1 mile per minute. What was the tornado's displacement? What was the tornado's average velocity?

Tornadoes form when warm air currents meet much cooler air currents. These conditions can produce thunderclouds and storms, and create a wind shear where the currents meet that causes the air to swirl. As the storm develops, the swirling air can increase, and eventually it may form a tornado.

Tornadoes are the most unpredictable of all storms. They often form quickly, leaving people with no time to prepare for them. Tornado winds are the strongest of all storm winds, sometimes exceeding 300 miles (483 km) per hour. A tornado spinning this quickly can knock over trees and buildings. It can also pick up and throw debris with great force. Most tornadoes are weak and cause little or no damage, but some tornadoes have been known to pick

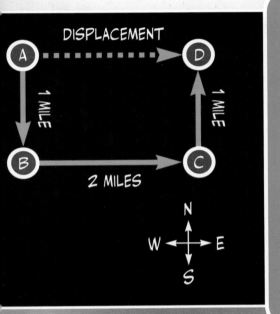

DISPLACEMENT

A · · · · · · · · · · · · ▶ D

1 MILE

B ──────────▶ C

2 MILES

1 MILE

N
W ◀─┼─▶ E
S

Since the tornado made 2 turns, we need to measure the distance from point A (beginning) to point D (ending) to find the tornado's displacement. The tornado's displacement was 2 miles. Now, let's use the formula for average velocity to find the tornado's average velocity.

$$v = \frac{\text{displacement}}{\text{time}}$$

$$v = \frac{2 \text{ miles}}{4 \text{ minutes}}$$

$$v = 0.5 \text{ mile/minute}$$

The velocity of the tornado was 0.5 mile per minute, east.

# HURRICANES

Hurricanes are severe storms capable of causing the most damage of any storm. Hurricanes are much larger than tornadoes and can last for over a week. They form over tropical ocean waters that are at least 80°F (27°C). At this temperature, the warm water **evaporates** quickly. This moisture forms storm clouds. As winds begin to increase, the hurricane begins to form as a wide thunderstorm. Soon this storm takes on a circular shape. Unlike tornadoes, hurricanes cannot form if wind shears occur. Hurricanes need stable, warm winds to develop.

Once the swirling winds reach 74 miles (119 km) per hour or more, the storm has become a hurricane. Hurricane winds can reach speeds up to 200 miles (322 km) per hour. The center of a hurricane traps the warmest air. This warm air creates an area called the eye where there are no clouds and no rain. The eye is usually 10 to 20 miles (16 to 32 km) in diameter. Immediately around the eye is the eye wall, a thick, dark band of clouds where the most damaging winds occur. Hurricane winds and clouds reach more than 200 miles (322 km) away from the eye. Severe hurricanes can have a diameter of about 500 miles (805 km). Hurricanes begin to break up once they move over land.

A hurricane has 2 velocities. The hurricane-wind velocity measures the swirling winds, which move counterclockwise in the Northern Hemisphere and clockwise in the Southern Hemisphere. The storm-center velocity measures the whole hurricane as it moves forward.

27

At 8:00 a.m. on September 10, 1999, Hurricane Floyd formed in the Atlantic Ocean. This huge storm battered the tiny islands of the Bahamas and then headed for the east coast of Florida. Floyd unexpectedly turned north and headed up the eastern coast of the United States. On September 16 at 2:30 a.m., Floyd hit land near Cape Fear, North Carolina. The storm had weakened by this point, but it still caused 56 deaths in the United States and billions of dollars in property damages. Floyd was downgraded to a tropical storm off the coast of Delaware after 11:00 a.m. on September 16, 1999, more than 6 days after it formed.

This map shows the path of Hurricane Floyd from the time it formed to the time it weakened to a tropical storm. From beginning to end, Floyd lasted a total of 150 hours. Use the information

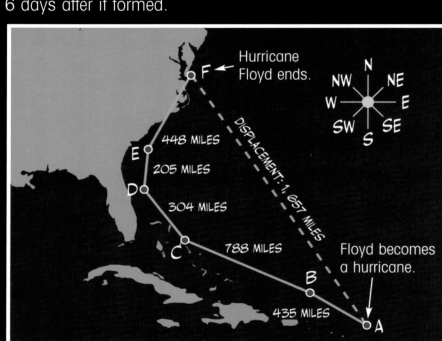

on this map to find out the following facts about Hurricane Floyd: total distance traveled, average speed, displacement, and average velocity.

To find the total distance that Floyd covered, add all the segments of its path.

$$
\begin{array}{r}
435 \text{ miles} \\
788 \text{ miles} \\
304 \text{ miles} \\
205 \text{ miles} \\
+ 448 \text{ miles} \\
\hline
2{,}180 \text{ miles}
\end{array}
$$

Floyd traveled a total distance of 2,180 miles. We can now use this value to calculate Floyd's average speed. Round your answer to the nearest tenth.

$$S = \frac{d}{t}$$

$$S = \frac{2{,}180 \text{ miles}}{150 \text{ hours}}$$

$$
\begin{array}{r}
14.53 \text{ miles per hour} \\
150 \,\overline{)2180.00} \\
-150 \phantom{00000} \\
\hline
680 \phantom{0000} \\
-600 \phantom{0000} \\
\hline
80\,0 \phantom{00} \\
-75\,0 \phantom{00} \\
\hline
5\,00 \phantom{0} \\
-4\,50 \phantom{0} \\
\hline
50 \phantom{0}
\end{array}
$$

Floyd's average speed was about 14.5 miles per hour.

To find Floyd's displacement, we need to measure the distance from its starting point to its ending point. If you look at the map, you will see that the displacement was 1,657 miles. Use this information to find Floyd's average velocity. Round your answer to the nearest mile. Don't forget the direction.

$$v = \frac{\text{displacement}}{\text{time}}$$

$$v = \frac{1{,}657 \text{ miles}}{150 \text{ hours}}$$

$$
\begin{array}{r}
11.04 \text{ miles per hour} \\
150 \,\overline{)1657.00} \\
-150 \phantom{0000} \\
\hline
157 \phantom{000} \\
-150 \phantom{000} \\
\hline
7\,00 \phantom{0} \\
-6\,00 \phantom{0} \\
\hline
1\,00 \phantom{0}
\end{array}
$$

Hurricane Floyd's average velocity was about 11 miles per hour, northwest.

29

# SEVERE STORMS IN THE SOLAR SYSTEM

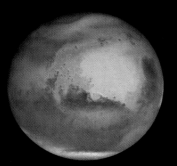

JUNE 26, 2001

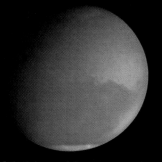

SEPTEMBER 4, 2001

These photos show the effects of a global dust storm that occurred on the planet Mars in 2001. The second image shows how the dust from the storm blocked most of the sunlight from the surface of Mars.

Meteorologists depend on tools like anemometers and Doppler radar to predict where and when severe storms will hit. This allows people to prepare for the storm and helps save lives. If meteorologists did not understand how to calculate velocity, they would not be able to do their jobs.

Earth isn't the only planet in the solar system that experiences severe storms. Mars experiences the most severe dust storms in the solar system. Dust storms have been known to hide the entire planet behind a veil of red dust. Jupiter features the largest hurricane-like storm in the solar system. This storm is more than 3 times the width of Earth! Jupiter's giant red spot is a swirling storm that has been circling the planet for as long as we have had telescopes strong enough to see it. This might be because there is no land for the storm to move over and break it up. Without being able to calculate velocity, scientists would not know as much as they do about these severe storms. Scientists continue to study the information they receive about storms on other planets to help them learn more about weather on Earth.

# GLOSSARY

**acceleration** (ihk-seh-luh-RAY-shun)  The rate of change in speed over time.

**antenna** (an-TEH-nuh)  A metal device such as a rod or wire that sends and receives radio waves.

**atmosphere** (AT-muh-sfeer)  The layer of air surrounding a planet.

**concentric** (kuhn-SEN-trik)  Having a common center.

**erosion** (ih-ROH-zhun)  The process of wearing away by the action of wind, water, or ice.

**evaporate** (ih-VA-puh-rayt)  To change from liquid into vapor.

**formula** (FOHR-myuh-luh)  A mathematical rule expressed in the form of an equation.

**instantaneous** (in-stuhn-TAY-nee-uhs)  Occurring at a particular moment.

**magnitude** (MAG-nuh-tood)  A measurement of size or extent.

**precipitation** (pruh-sih-puh-TAY-shun)  Any form of water falling from the sky, including rain, snow, sleet, freezing rain, and hail.

**scalar quantity** (SKAY-luhr KWAHN-tuh-tee)  A value that can be expressed by size or extent alone.

**vector quantity** (VEHK-tuhr KWAHN-tuh-tee)  A value that is expressed by magnitude and direction.

**vegetation** (veh-juh-TAY-shun)  Plant life.

**visibility** (vih-zuh-BIH-luh-tee)  The farthest distance one can see.

**wind turbine** (WIND TUHR-byn)  A machine with blades that turn with the wind. This motion is used to create electrical energy.

31

# INDEX